ANIMALS
That Make a Difference!

Koalas

Ashley Lee

Explore other books at:
WWW.ENGAGEBOOKS.COM

VANCOUVER, B.C.

e WWW.ENGAGEBOOKS.COM

Koalas: Pre-1
Animals That Make a Difference!
Lee, Ashley, 1995
Text © 2025 Engage Books
Design © 2025 Engage Books

Edited by: A.R. Roumanis, and Ashley Lee
Design by: Mandy Christiansen

Text set in Arial Regular.

FIRST EDITION / FIRST PRINTING

library and archives canada cataloguing in publication

Title: Koalas / Ashley Lee.
Names: Lee, Ashley, author.
Description: Series statement: Animals that make a difference

Identifiers: Canadiana (print) 20230448542 | Canadiana (ebook) 20230448569
ISBN 978-1-77878-689-1 (hardcover)
ISBN 978-1-77878-698-3 (softcover)

Subjects:
LCSH: Koalas—Juvenile literature.
LCSH: Human-animal relationships—Juvenile literature.

Classification: LCC QL737.P94 C38 2025 | DDC J599.885—DC23

This project has been made possible in part
by the Government of Canada.

Canada

What is hiding
in that tree?

Koalas are sometimes called koala bears.

But koalas are
not bears.

Koalas have a pouch on their belly.

They have two thumbs on each hand.

Koalas live in Australia.

They live in trees.

9

Koalas sleep for about 20 hours every day.

11

Koalas only eat one kind of plant.

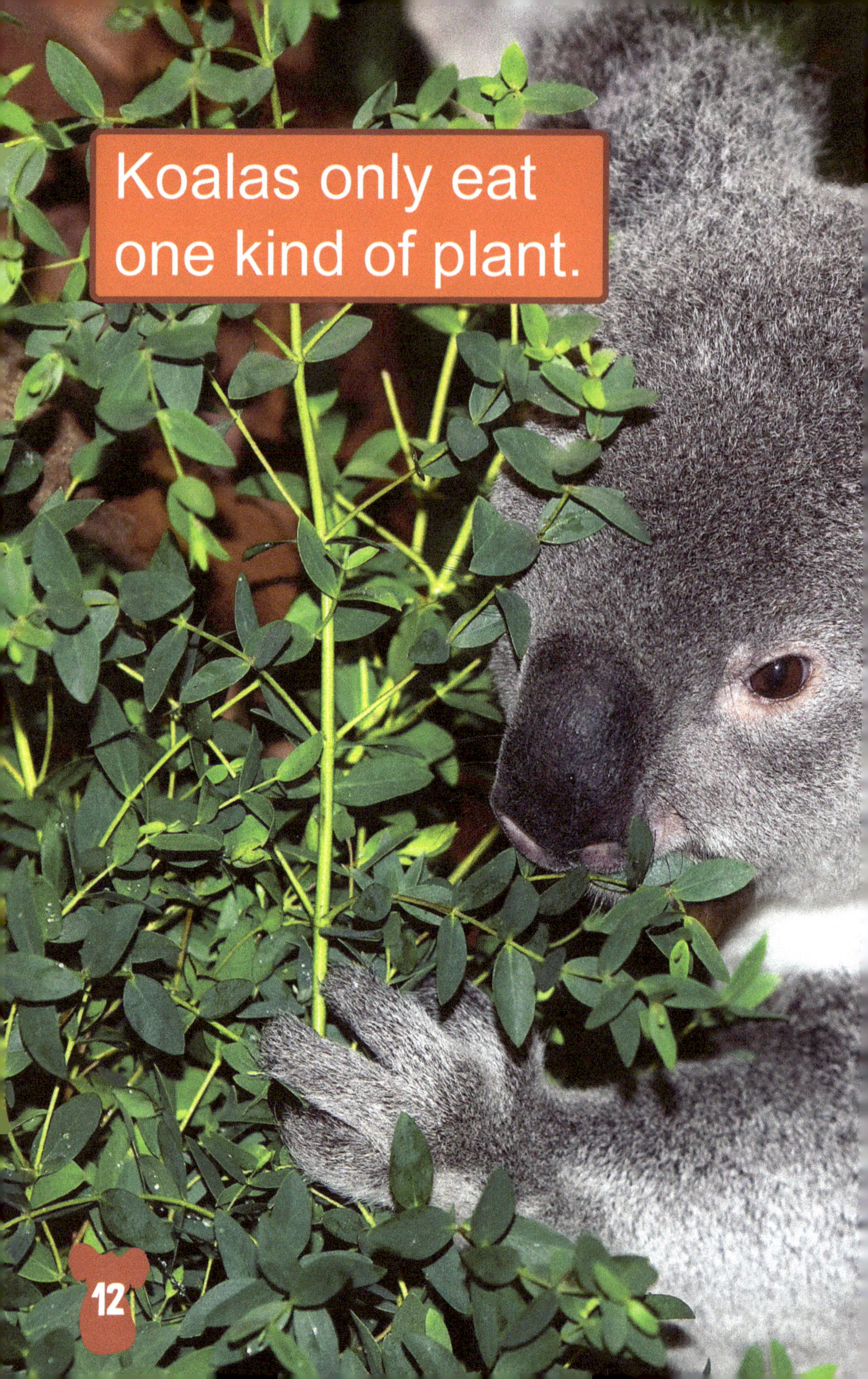

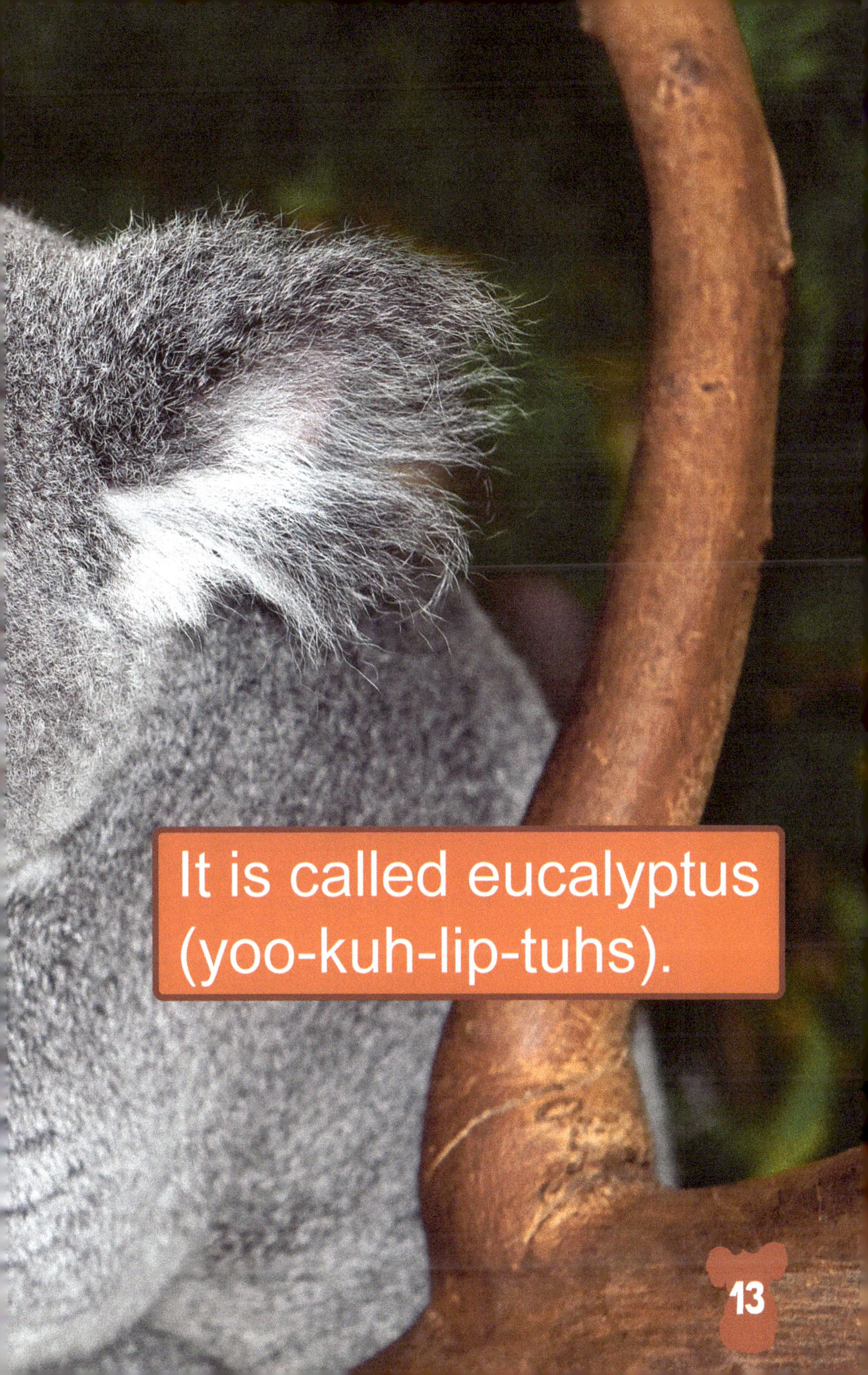

It is called eucalyptus (yoo-kuh-lip-tuhs).

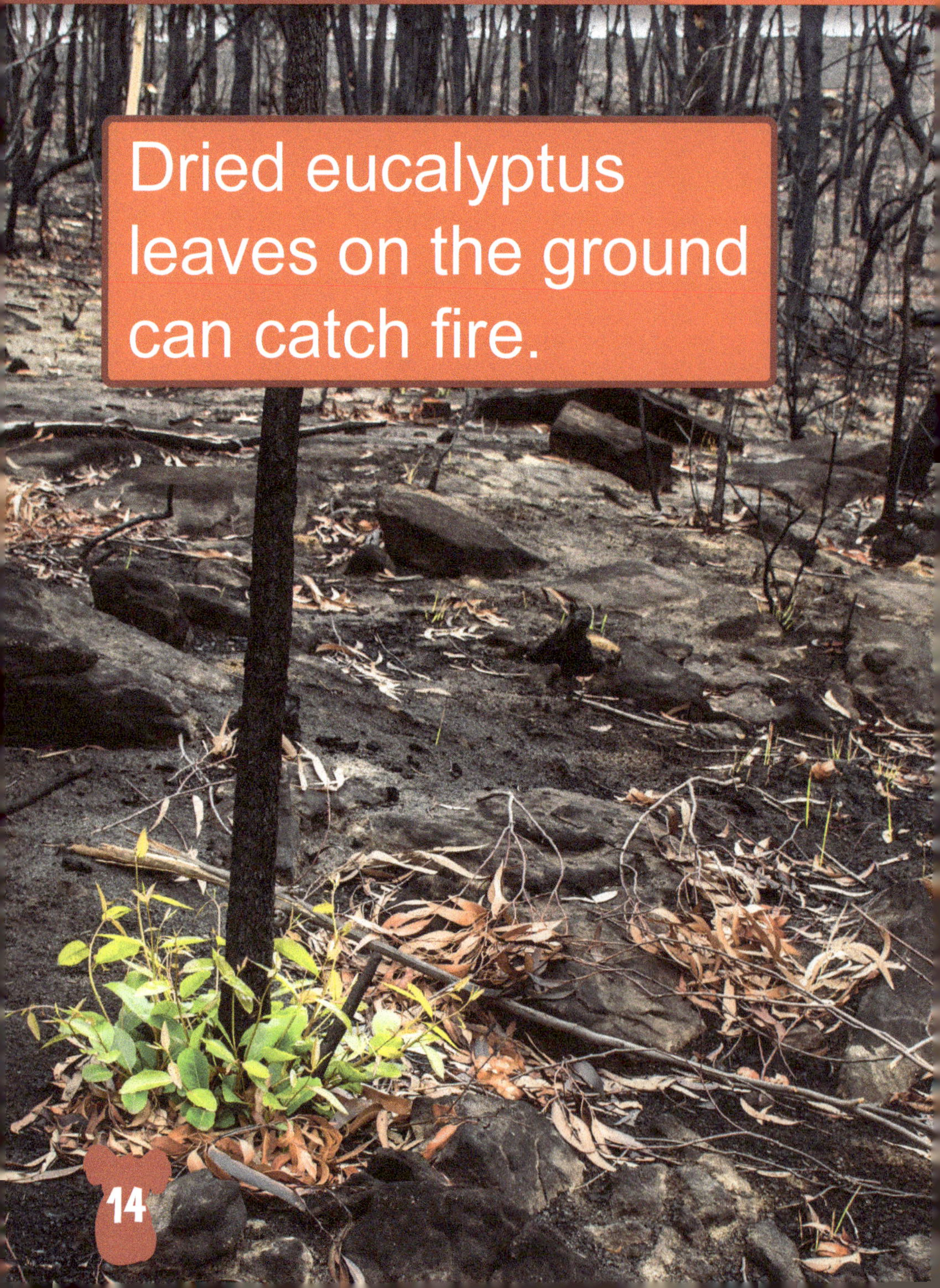

Dried eucalyptus leaves on the ground can catch fire.

Eating leaves helps stop fires from spreading.

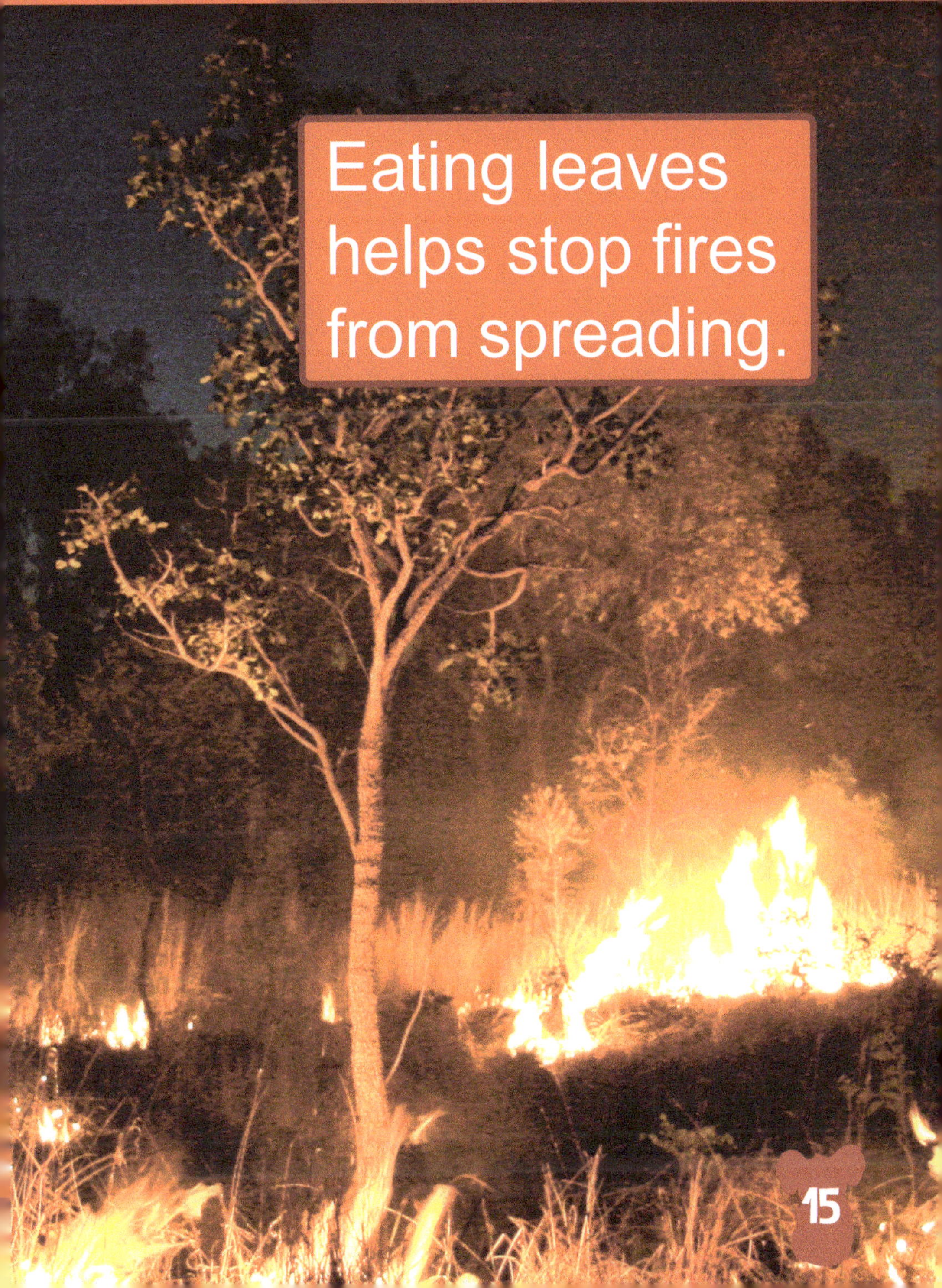

Eucalyptus trees can stop sunlight from reaching other plants.

Eating leaves lets sunlight reach other plants.

Sunlight helps plants grow.

19

Koalas often have
one baby at a time.

Babies are the size
of a jelly bean.

Mothers keep their babies in their belly pouch until they get bigger.

Koalas are in danger.

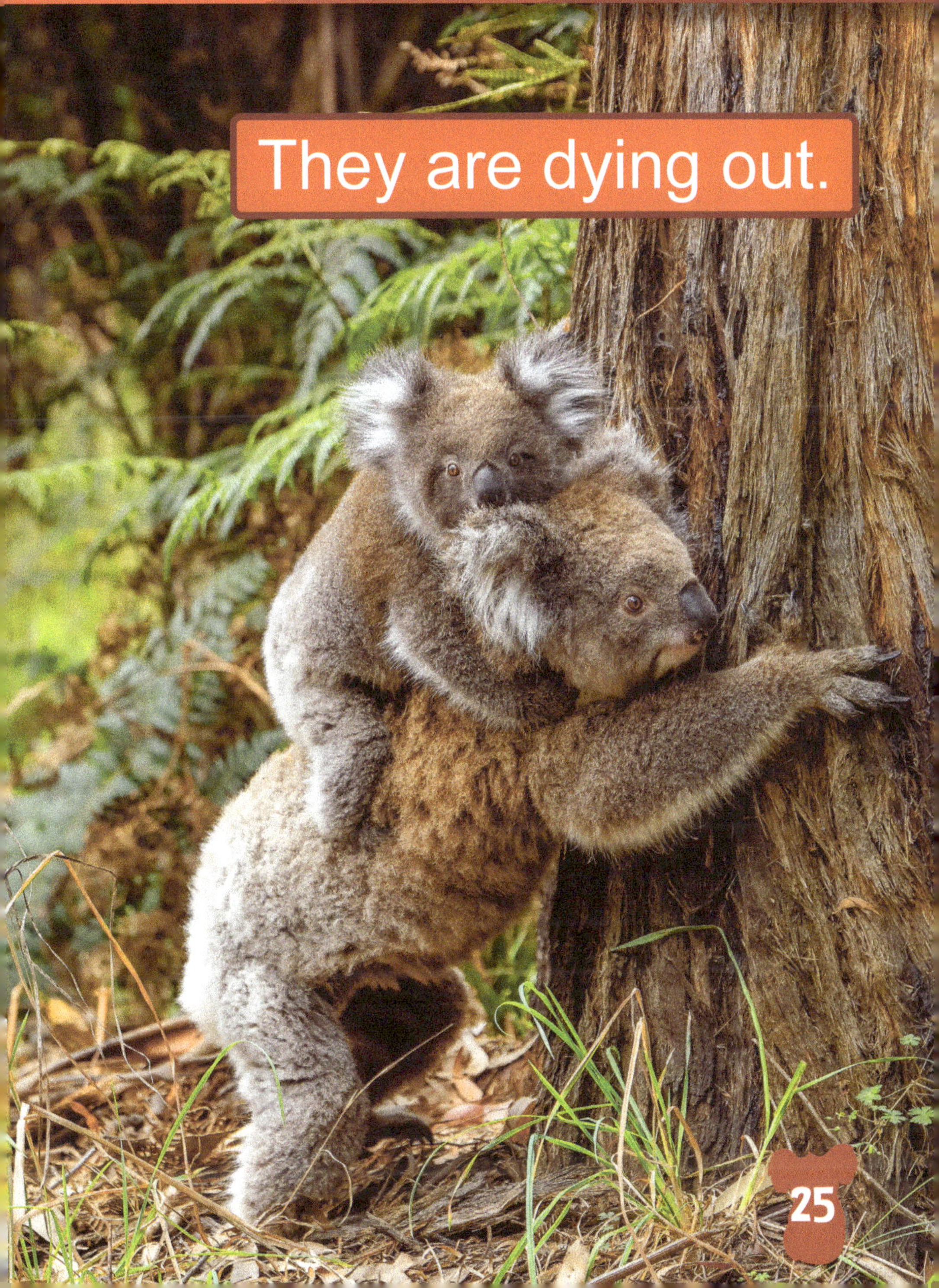

They are dying out.

People are cutting down their forests.

Wildfires are burning the trees.

But people can help koalas.

People are planting trees and fighting forest fires.

Quiz

Test your knowledge of koalas by answering the following questions. The questions are based on what you have read in this book. The answers are listed on the bottom of the next page.

1 Are koalas bears?

2 Do koalas have two thumbs on each hand?

3 Do koalas live in trees?

4 Do koalas often have one baby at a time?

5 Are koalas in danger?

6 Can people help koalas?

Explore other books in the
Animals That Make a Difference series

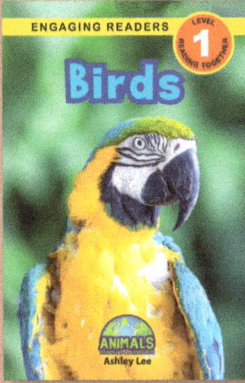

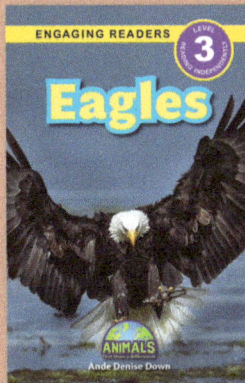

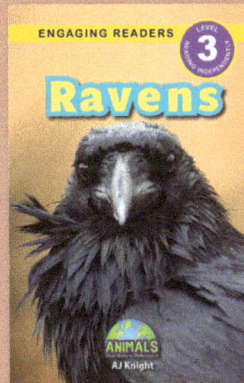

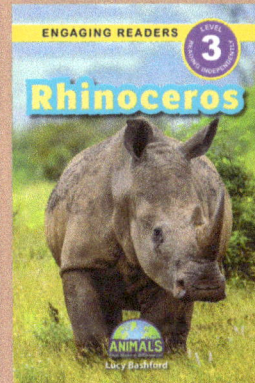

ENGAGING READERS — LEVEL 1
Birds
Ashley Lee

ENGAGING READERS — LEVEL 1
Ladybugs
Ashley Lee

ENGAGING READERS — LEVEL 1
Squirrels
Ashley Lee

ENGAGING READERS — LEVEL 2
Butterflies
Ashley Lee

ENGAGING READERS — LEVEL 2
Frogs
Ashley Lee

ENGAGING READERS — LEVEL 2
Octopuses
Ashley Lee

ENGAGING READERS — LEVEL 3
Eagles
Ande Denise Down

ENGAGING READERS — LEVEL 3
Ravens
AJ Knight

ENGAGING READERS — LEVEL 3
Rhinoceros
Lucy Bashford

Visit www.engagebooks.com to explore more Engaging Readers.

www.ingramcontent.com/pod-product-compliance
Lightning Source LLC
Chambersburg PA
CBHW052035030426
42337CB00027B/5023